The BOOSEY & HAWKES

TRUMPET

OLOGY

13 composers

3/12

BOOSEY & HAWKES

DISTRIBUTED BY

HAL•LEONARD®
CORPORATION

7777 W. BLUEMOUND RD. P.O. BOX 13819 MILWAUKEE, WI 53213

www.boosey.com
www.halleonard.com

CONTENTS

* for unaccompanied Trumpet(s), please see the inserted Trumpet part.

Fanfare and Berceuse

ARTHUR BUTTERWORTH

Fanfare

* concert pitch

Berceuse

Larghetto

Red, White and Blues

LEONARD BERNSTEIN

Slow, heavy blues tempo

Tpt.*
(in B-flat)

mf freely (as in blues singing)

Pno.

mf

f sub.

f sub.

* concert pitch

For my brother Burtie

Rondo for Lifey*

LEONARD BERNSTEIN

* Lifey is Judy Holliday's Skye terrier.

** concert pitch

14

A Simple Song
from *Mass*

Arranged for trumpet and piano by
DAVID J. ELLIOT

LEONARD BERNSTEIN

* concert pitch

Zion's Walls

from *Old American Songs, Set 2*

Arranged for trumpet and piano by
QUINCY C. HILLIARD

AARON COPLAND

* concert pitch

Quiet City

Arranged for trumpet and piano by
PETER WASTALL

AARON COPLAND

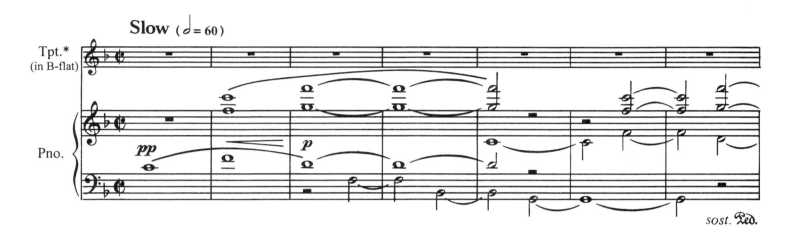

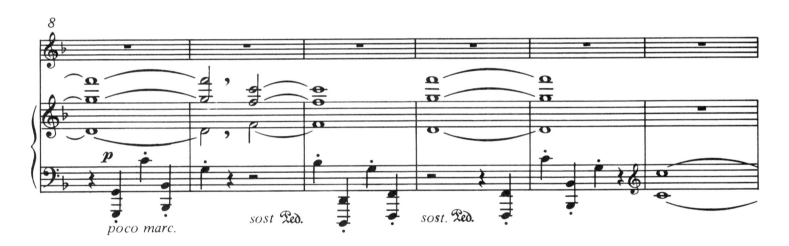

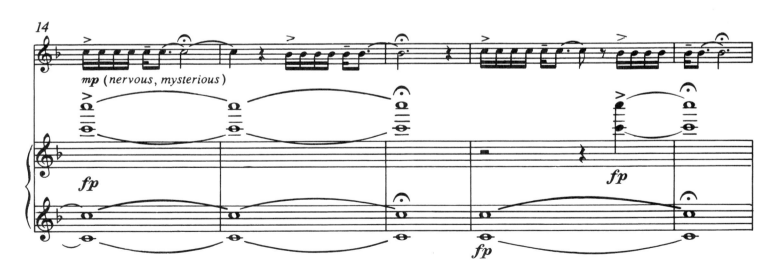

The original version of 'Quiet City' for trumpet, English horn (or oboe) and string orchestra is available on hire from the publishers.

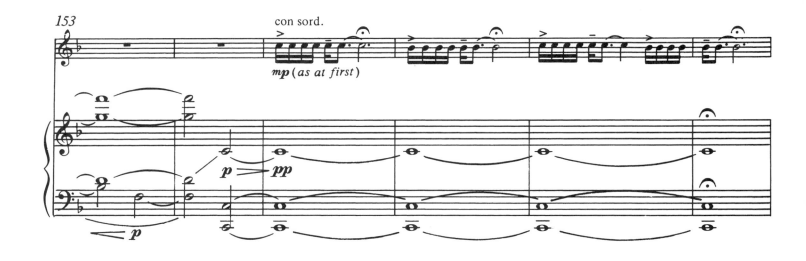

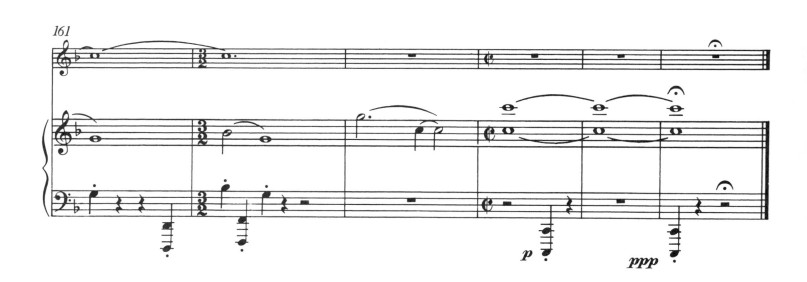

Billy and His Sweetheart
from *Billy the Kid*

Arranged for trumpet and piano by
QUINCY C. HILLIARD

AARON COPLAND

* concert pitch

** The solo part has occasionally been displaced by an octave.

34

Enjoying Life

IVAN ERÖD

* concert pitch

Conversation

CLARE GRUNDMAN

* concert pitch

40

Slicked Back Tango

ELENA KATS - CHERNIN

(some liberties may be taken with the piano part regarding the addition of octave doublings, pedalling, and ornamentation)

* concert pitch

21 June 2002
Coogee, Sydney

for Tony, Gareth and Ian Small, 'Trumpets Three'

Salm o Dewi Sant

KARL JENKINS

* concert pitch

48

Cries and Whispers

NED ROREM

54

March 2000

Fantasy Piece

KURT SCHWERTSIK

* concert pitch

Serenade

KURT SCHWERTSIK

Rhapsody
(for Trumpet and Band or Orchestra)

FISHER TULL

* concert pitch

* Optional cut: ⌐   ⌐

To John J. Haynie
Commissioned by his students in recognition of his 25 years
as professor of trumpet at North Texas State University

Three Bagatelles

I. Prelude

FISHER TULL

* concert pitch

88

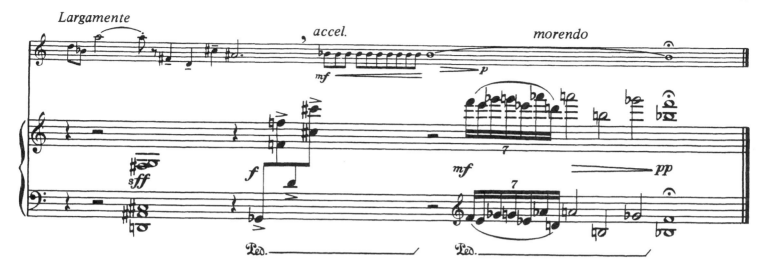

II. Improvisation

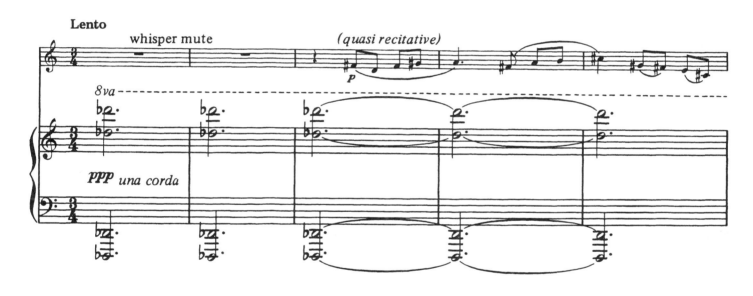

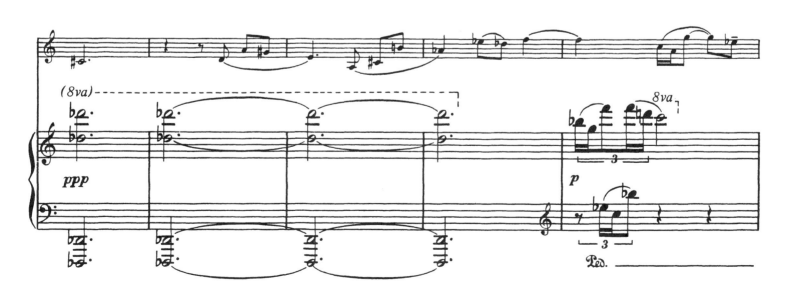

III. Caprice